69+1 Ways to enjoy your life during a
pandemic quarantine and to preserve your
mental health

ISBN: 978-0-9743273-3-4

Published in Houston, Texas 4/2020
Publisher: Shaykobi Destiny Resources

69+1 Ways to enjoy your life during a
pandemic quarantine and to preserve your
mental health

69+1 Ways to enjoy your life during a pandemic quarantine and to preserve your mental health

Dedication

This book is dedicated to Kobe Bryant. My heart goes out to the Bryant family. I have adored Kobe Bryant for many years, as a fan. Seeing his great talents, ability to pull a team together and even his ability to mess up personally and to own it and work things through was priceless. I named my son after him, hoping that he would one day stand in his own greatness. Watching Kobe on the court or in video snippet's with his family really showed his heart and talent. I most remember when The Lakers were here in Houston playing The Rockets. Yes, I go with the home team, except for when Kobe was involved. I couldn't take my eyes off of him as he appeared to be a team of one sometimes. The way that he moved with quickness and such precision didn't even seem real, yet I knew it was. His greatness and blessings were felt wherever he went. He was the epitome of what a great father is. We've certainly had some great athletes in all era's. For me, Kobe has always been like a pot full of gold at the end of a

69+1 Ways to enjoy your life during a pandemic quarantine and to preserve your mental health

rainbow-valuable, hoped for, expected, wished for, a dream and desired by many for many different reasons. Kobe, we love you and miss you-the world misses you.

69+1 Ways to enjoy your life during a pandemic quarantine and to preserve your mental health

Introduction

This is an unusual time for anyone in every country across the globe. This is a time of unity while being a time of separation and support. It's so important to have human connections albeit via technology. As we read the headlines about the emerging and trending Covid-19, coronavirus, SARS and begin to watch all of the scary video segments about 5G, who can sleep and who can eat?

The idea of this book came about as I have been conducting my usual psychotherapy with my clients and many of them have reported not knowing what to do while working from home or being laid off due to the current outbreak. To some of them, I suggested sitting down and coming up with a list of things to do.

We should be mindful that as this pandemic is happening many other changes are affecting our lives: family members dying from natural causes, all of our school aged kids are at home, working from home or waiting to be called back to work post coronavirus 19,

69+1 Ways to enjoy your life during a pandemic quarantine and to preserve your mental health

relationship difficulties, the mortgage or rent is still due, the electric bill, car notes and more. Bleach, toilet tissue and many other items remain scarce whether shopping big box wholesalers or the local mom and pop grocery store. This is adding to individual anxiety let alone the anxiety that is multiplied with several people living in a home together.

69+1 Ways to enjoy your life during a pandemic quarantine and to preserve your mental health

FAQ's

Should I tell my children about Covid-19?
Because of all of the hype centered around Covid-19, it could be traumatic and harmful to tell your child under 14 about it. I explained it to a child and shared that some people have a bug (i.e. virus) that makes them not feel too well. Because of this, we have to keep our distance.

What types of things should I share with my child(ren) about it?
For young people 14 and under, you can explain that in the world there are different kinds of sicknesses. Lately some people in different places have been sick. Because of that, we are taking some precautions to remain well and not to spread the illness.

What do I need to know about Covid 19?

It's here and like the cold, a coronavirus and the flu, a coronavirus, it is here to stay. Also, like the flu, a vaccine is in the works at this moment to reduce human demise and to increase the efficacy of input from the medical

69+1 Ways to enjoy your life during a pandemic quarantine and to preserve your mental health

community to not just fight but to prevent future outbreaks of this virus, the 19th version of a coronavirus. While some people have died, there have been less deaths at the time of this printing than deaths via the flu despite having a vaccine. If you are under 60 and don't have comorbid, pre-existing medical conditions, the likelihood of suffering demise at the behest of the virus has proven to be lower than it would for a well person under 60. Young people without underlying conditions have died. At this moment, 533,378 people have tested positive in the US. There have been 20,601 deaths and 32,026 recoveries. Globally, as of this moment there have been nearly 2 million confirmed cases, 411,836 recoveries and 109,823 deaths.

What can I do to help reduce the spread of the virus?

While many people are running around in an anxious state, that really isn't helpful to the people themselves nor to their family. You can help to reduce transmission by doing the following things:

69+1 Ways to enjoy your life during a pandemic quarantine and to preserve your mental health

It spreads:

- There is currently no vaccine to prevent coronavirus disease 2019 (COVID-19).
- The best way to prevent illness is to avoid being exposed to this virus.
- The virus is thought to spread mainly from person-to-person.
  - Between people who are in close contact with one another (within about 6 feet).
  - Through respiratory droplets produced when an infected person coughs or sneezes.
- These droplets can land in the mouths or noses of people who are nearby or possibly be inhaled into the lungs.

To protect yourself:

Clean your hands often

- Wash your hands often with soap and water for at least 20 seconds especially after you have been in a public place, or after blowing your nose, coughing, or sneezing.

69+1 Ways to enjoy your life during a pandemic quarantine and to preserve your mental health

- If soap and water are not readily available, use a hand sanitizer that contains at least 60% alcohol. Cover all surfaces of your hands and rub them together until they feel dry.
- Avoid touching your eyes, nose, and mouth with unwashed hands.

Avoid close contact

- Avoid close contact with people who are sick
- Put distance between yourself and other people if COVID-19 is spreading in your community. This is especially important for people who are at higher risk of getting very sick.
- Stay home if you are sick, except to get medical care. Learn what to do if you are sick.

Cover coughs and sneezes

- Cover your mouth and nose with a tissue when you cough or sneeze or use the inside of your elbow.
- Throw used tissues in the trash.

69+1 Ways to enjoy your life during a pandemic quarantine and to preserve your mental health

- Immediately wash your hands with soap and water for at least 20 seconds. If soap and water are not readily available,

- clean your hands with a hand sanitizer that contains at least 60% alcohol.

Wear a facemask if you are or aren't sick

- If you are sick: You should wear a facemask when you are around other people (e.g., sharing a room or vehicle) and before you enter a healthcare provider's office. If you are not able to wear a facemask (for example, because it causes trouble breathing), then you should do your best to cover your coughs and sneezes, and people who are caring for you should wear a facemask if they enter your room. Learn what to do if you are sick.
- If you are NOT sick: Still wear a facemask. Facemasks may be in short supply and they should be saved for caregivers/ front-line workers.
- By the time you are reading this book, some phenomenal people have made

69+1 Ways to enjoy your life during a
pandemic quarantine and to preserve your
mental health

masks at home and have sent them to
first responders. Many companies have
taken on a new purpose such as making

- hand sanitizer and face shields along
  with other PPE.

Clean and disinfect

- Clean AND disinfect frequently touched
  surfaces daily. This includes tables,
  doorknobs, light switches, countertops,
  handles, desks, phones, keyboards,
  toilets, faucets, and sinks.
- If surfaces are dirty, clean them: Use
  detergent or soap and water prior to
  disinfection.

To disinfect:

Most common EPA-registered household
disinfectants will work. Use disinfectants
appropriate for the surface.

Options include:

- Diluting your household bleach.
  To make a bleach solution, mix:

69+1 Ways to enjoy your life during a pandemic quarantine and to preserve your mental health

- 5 tablespoons (1/3rd cup) bleach per gallon of water
  OR
- 4 teaspoons bleach per quart of water
- Follow manufacturer's instructions for application and proper ventilation. Check to ensure the product is not past its expiration date. Never mix household bleach with ammonia or any other cleanser. Unexpired household bleach will be effective against coronaviruses when properly diluted.
- Alcohol solutions.
  Ensure the solution has at least 70% alcohol.
- Other common EPA-registered household disinfectants.
  Products with EPA-approved emerging viral pathogens
- claims are expected to be effective against COVID-19 based on data for harder to kill viruses. Follow the manufacturer's instructions for all cleaning and disinfection products (e.g.,

69+1 Ways to enjoy your life during a pandemic quarantine and to preserve your mental health

concentration, application method and contact time, etc.).

The News

We saw it happen with 9/11, the new media wouldn't stop showing graphic pictures. They reported on that event for what seemed to be an eternity. Day in and day out people watched in dismay and fear and ultimately developed an uncertainty about life in America. They began to question their safety and how these events would affect America, their freedoms and how they lived in general.

To see the event once was traumatizing let alone seeing it on the news cycle, morning, news and night. Nowadays, with cell phones, watch phones, other tablets, laptops, desktops, smart televisions and the like along with push notifications, it seems inevitable that you will be exposed to information that can be overwhelming.

69+1 Ways to enjoy your life during a pandemic quarantine and to preserve your mental health

Learning about Covid-19 throughout 90% of each news report has different effects on many people. Some of my own clients have reported: anxiety, breaking out in sweats, inability to sleep after watching the news, an inability to

focus, a fear of the unknown and more. Because it's everywhere, they struggle with disconnecting.

<u>Disconnecting</u>

I recently disconnected by turning notifications down. I have missed several phone calls and texts. Because I chose not to be ruled by my phone or television, I felt better and amazingly, no one died because I didn't answer a call or didn't respond to a text in 30 minutes.

If you can, order groceries online and either have them delivered or pick them up. Prepare in the event the supply chain is disrupted. Top items would include a first aid kit, canned and frozen goods, a manual can opener, napkins, toilet tissue, water, candles, any usual medications that you take regularly.

69+1 Ways to enjoy your life during a pandemic quarantine and to preserve your mental health

1. Reading
2. Prayer
3. Walking/Jogging outdoors
4. Mindfulness
5. Meditation

6. Exercise/Stretching
7. Talking with friends and family/video chats
8. Cleaning house
9. Teaching kids that are home from school
10. Make a list of fun things you can do while at home alone or with family (who lives with you)

69+1 Ways to enjoy your life during a pandemic quarantine and to preserve your mental health

Foreword

While you will be able to read the list of things that you can do as they are here in this book, you will also think of additional things that aren't here. You should add them to the list. You should send me a message so that I can add them to the list.

Throughout this book, you will see pictures that I have taken with a Google Pixel 3 phone and have adjusted with my untrained eye. These pictures were taken during my walks which caused me to feel relaxed and at peace during the Covid-19 situation. I've found that in taking these pictures, I've been more mindful about the beauty around me and thus adding more hope and joy to my personal treasure box. I

69+1 Ways to enjoy your life during a
pandemic quarantine and to preserve your
mental health
hope that you will find the same in looking at
them.

How eloquent. The photo looks like a painting.

69+1 Ways to enjoy your life during a pandemic quarantine and to preserve your mental health

1. Have a Corona beer (Lol)

The first thing that you should know is that I don't really promote drinking but if you enjoy Corona, or Michelob Ultra is my favorite-you should relax and have one from time to time. If you're on Keto, Michelob Ultra has a very low carb count and it tastes divine. If you're from New Orleans or Maine you might want to have that with crawfish or lobster. In other parts of the country or the world, you might just have one while talking with friends or over a game of checkers or poker. When was the last time you played a game of checkers or chess?

69+1 Ways to enjoy your life during a pandemic quarantine and to preserve your mental health

69+1 Ways to enjoy your life during a pandemic quarantine and to preserve your mental health

2. *Put a picnic blanket outside while reading an interesting book*

Some of us are getting all wound up instead of having a picnic at home. You can do it in an apartment as well. All you need is a blanket, a fly swatter if it's hot and you plan to have some delicious potato salad and fried chicken. Or maybe your snack will be more regal: grapes, cheese and crackers. What about that? You can have whatever your heart desires, but in all that you have, have a relaxing time. You can fire up your favorite music playlist, watch your kids play, enjoy nature, talk with your significant other and if you live alone, you can have a friend to join you online to picnic together. How does that sound? I know it's not your usual picnic, but it can lift your spirits and reduce your stress at the same time.

3. *Send your friends an electronic invite to an online party*

This one, I shared with a client before it was even shared on the news that people were busting this move. We can go over to our friends homes and potentially harm them or be harmed or just send out that invite and wait for everyone who is cool and happening to accept then the party is on. Remember, people can be carriers and appear 100% well. It's not about being afraid, it's about being prepared and making smart moves for yourself and your future.

69+1 Ways to enjoy your life during a pandemic quarantine and to preserve your mental health

69+1 Ways to enjoy your life during a
pandemic quarantine and to preserve your
mental health

4. *Go and take a daily jog before everyone gets on the track*

A jog or a walk can be quite nice. Usually I will listen to inspirational videos on YouTube while I'm taking my trek. Today, I was on the phone with an ex. I will say we're good friends and we had a perfect conversation the entire 45 minutes. So, you can listen to music, talk to a friend or someone who won't increase your blood pressure or stress level or just enjoy the peace and quiet of nature. Remember, if you are passing others, take your proper distance to protect yourself and the other person. Remember, exercise 3x per week has a great potential of keeping the doctor away, especially if you are eating well too.

69+1 Ways to enjoy your life during a pandemic quarantine and to preserve your mental health

5. Watch a few shows on Netflix, Hulu, Apple TV, Amazon Prime or other lovely apps

I know that you've heard being a couch potato isn't good, but it's good for all of us to take a load off sometimes. Loving what I do so much, sometimes I have to make myself disconnect to relax and often something great on Amazon Prime, Netflix Apple TV or Hulu meets my need for something funny, a documentary, a love story and with my granddaughter, an animated show. So, it doesn't matter what you like, you can find it. Most of the apps have some original shows that you will certainly enjoy as well.

6. Cook dinner with your family (that you live with)

If you live alone, you can cook with a friend online. Otherwise, you can involve the loved ones that you live with. I often include my granddaughter for cracking eggs, stirring something or shaping Keto Chocolate Chip Cookies (Chocolate Covered Katie-to die for) and more. Besides that, you can get everyone to take a part, from setting places at the table, to washing the dishes afterwards and even having different people make different parts of the meal. If you want, you can have some background music that will still allow you to have conversations and to listen to the instructions of the master chef in the home. Lol.

69+1 Ways to enjoy your life during a pandemic quarantine and to preserve your mental health

7. Send out an electronic invite to have a cooking competition and login at the appropriate time

I would say that you want to talk to the people that you plan to invite first, then send them out an invite. Make sure that you have the rules established and each person has to have at least two people besides themselves in the household to score the dishes. It could even be streamed live on YouTube or FaceBook and that would cause quite a stir. Commence to cooking, peeking over at Zoom or Microsoft Meetings to see what your competition is doing and please talk sh*t. That makes it really good.

69+1 Ways to enjoy your life during a
pandemic quarantine and to preserve your
mental health

69+1 Ways to enjoy your life during a pandemic quarantine and to preserve your mental health

8. **Reflect on your life and decide on ways you can improve and be better, begin implementing the plans today**

For some of us, it can be a challenge to look within ourselves or to be introspective. This is a good practice to have. We will remain the same in life or become better through being introspective. We should be growing and evolving. I'm wondering how much I've grown or evolved since I was a kid. I was writing poetry at a young age and many people don't even know me, which is fine. Does it mean that I haven't evolved because I'm still writing? Nope, it doesn't as this is a passion and will stick with me. If you can't find areas that could stand some growth or improvement, ask the 5 people you talk with the most. If no one can think of anything to say, it's probably your attitude that could use some adjusting. Lol.

69+1 Ways to enjoy your life during a
pandemic quarantine and to preserve your
mental health

9. *Play some video games and work at beating your best all time score*

While I'm old school and remember Atari
vividly, technology has become so much more
intelligent and now you can play with your body
or your hands. Years ago, when I played tennis
while burning some serious calories via a video
game, I thought that was amazing. Now people
are able to connect globally and have
counterparts who love the same game to play
with them. About this, please be safe and
make sure your kids are safe when they
connect with people. Preferably, anyone under
16 should be playing with people they know.
Find some great games that are age
appropriate for various family members and
enjoy some fun times.

10. Clean your house, one room at a time from the rooter to the tooter

As you've heard and read, cleaning can help to keep you and your family safer than if you didn't clean your home well. You can start with your front door, window seals, corners in rooms, spaces behind heavy furniture, all switches and knobs and then all of the general areas, one room at a time. This is not to suggest that you didn't already clean your home. The purpose of this activity is to impress upon you the seriousness of keeping the house clean to prevent the spread of the virus. It's even more important when you have people going in and out of your home.

69+1 Ways to enjoy your life during a
pandemic quarantine and to preserve your
mental health

11. Call a friend to discuss recent changes and how you can support each other at this time

While your friend might be a therapist, due to
ethical conflicts, they can't be your therapist.
You can both contact each other when you
would like to have a light-hearted chat. Maybe
you can help her by watching her kids via
FaceTime while she runs to the restroom. Who
knows? The main thing is to be there for each
other during a challenging time.

69+1 Ways to enjoy your life during a pandemic quarantine and to preserve your mental health

Do you see the little creature beside the water, near the grass?

69+1 Ways to enjoy your life during a pandemic quarantine and to preserve your mental health

12. Get a therapist that you can talk with to help you stay grounded during this time and other times

I have heard so many things said about psychotherapists over the years. One of the things that holds true is that: with the right therapist and you being fully invested in your wellness it's possible to have an excellent outcome if you do all that's required on your end. Therapy is a team of people, be it two or more that come together to help a person, a couple or family and sometimes a group to get from one place in their lives to another place. The actual goals are created with the therapist and conversations about those goals usually had overtime. The progress of those goals should be measured and discussed. Whether you're dealing with a pandemic like right now or any other time having a good therapist, someone who you can relate to is a benefit all the time. And if you choose a therapist and start off seeing them once per week the goal is that you eventually dwindle down to once per month where you're doing check-ins. CEOs,

69+1 Ways to enjoy your life during a pandemic quarantine and to preserve your mental health

famous people and others seek out therapy on a regular basis. They have huge responsibilities to the people they work for and that work for them and to audiences, producers and such. Many of us have responsibilities to our partners, families, employers and our communities. Having a great therapist in your life can save your life. A few great places to find therapists are: Psychology Today, Teladoc or BetterHelp. There are other sources like your insurance carrier websites and other apps.

69+1 Ways to enjoy your life during a
pandemic quarantine and to preserve your
mental health

13. Log on to YouTube and look up "Mindfulness Meditation" and get to work

Mindfulness meditation is relaxing. It helps to reduce stress and anxiety, reduces mild depression, helps you to become more centered, focused and grounded. You can get the whole family involved. You can begin to teach your toddler from a young age so that they can use the tool as they are growing up and in their adult life. There are many mindfulness apps like Headspace that are beneficial to millions around the globe.

14. *Learn a new hobby, instrument or language*

A new hobby is always something interesting to get into. It's very healthy to increase your knowledge base and to try new and positive things. If you have children, you guys can create a new experience together. If you do not have children, it will be something for you, you and your roommates, or you and your friends or spouse. If you feel like you don't know which hobby to try, look online because there's a lot of places that discuss different types of hobbies you can get into. Check out Duolingo for language learning for free or on a budget. For hobbies, there is even a site: www.discoverahobby.com.

69+1 Ways to enjoy your life during a
pandemic quarantine and to preserve your
mental health

15. Play board games with your family

Earlier I mentioned checkers. While checkers
is something that I've played over the years, I
think that my favorite board game has always
been Monopoly. I talk about Monopoly in my
book "10 ways to save and grow money." It
discusses how as a child you were learning
skills about money and life while playing it,
however, many of us have failed to transfer the
skills that we should have learned through
playing Monopoly. If someone doesn't know
how to play the game, there are always
instructions. If others know how to play it, they
can share how to play it with the others. Board
games can go from 10 minutes to hours long.
For Monopoly, you can literally play it for hours
and come back the next day. Something like
board games can really bring your family
together and open up positive communication.
All phones down. Some others are: Risk,
Scrabble, Pandemic, Clue, Backgammon,
Chess and so many more.

69+1 Ways to enjoy your life during a pandemic quarantine and to preserve your mental health

16. Play card games with your family

When I was a child my parents used to have and go to card games. As a child I used to sit back and play with other kids while the adults were playing cards. They laughed, maybe had a drink and even back then probably smoked a cigarette. I'm not suggesting that you play cards with your family and drink and smoke. I'm just sharing my own personal experience. The idea of playing cards always appeared really fun. Over the years we've enjoyed games like Spades, pitty-pat, as a kid - Go Fish, UNO and other games. While some people enjoy playing for money, we never really did that. Some people would play for pennies and that was interesting. So, if you have some cards in your home you are ready to begin. If not, perhaps you can call a friend or go online to figure out how to play some of these fun games as some of them can go on for hours on end.

69+1 Ways to enjoy your life during a pandemic quarantine and to preserve your mental health

17. Have a family barbeque at home and invite some friends to hang out electronically

There is nothing more fun than a good, old fashioned Texas barbeque. It's time to pull out the accessory for all-the cowboy hat. You have to pull out the pit and don't bring anything less than a brisket. Of course, barbeque means many things to different people. Growing up in Louisiana, barbeque was in the over or on a grill and barbeque sauce was mandatory. Living in Missouri, I learned that the sauce wasn't even considered until the last moment. I was told that it was often left out altogether. I was told that the main thing there was grilling the meat or veggies. I'm sure they had some, but while living in Virginia, I don't recall seeing any grills or smelling any food on a barbeque pit. Either way, If you like it with or without the sauce, have your food with folks and a side of fun. Don't forget the music.

69+1 Ways to enjoy your life during a pandemic quarantine and to preserve your mental health

No social distancing here.

69+1 Ways to enjoy your life during a
pandemic quarantine and to preserve your
mental health

18. Wash your car, truck, suv or suv want to be :)

Of course it's been raining on and off and most
recently snowing in some places.Even though
some of us aren't having to drive to work now,
it's a good time to give our vehicle a deep
cleaning. Life usually has us busy, especially if
you live in the U.S. Sometimes life seems
non-stop. So, turn your music on, get the water
and other supplies and go outside to enjoy
some sun. Wash your car inside and out.
Sanitize it. If you have kids, make it fun and
give them sponges as well.

19. Clean your gutters/siding/brick/ driveways

Who said everything in life was fun? The truth is, it may not be fun but it will help to extend their longevity. What do you think? This is a good job for teens to help with as well. You will need a ladder, gloves and a garbage can. You can put some music on, sing out loud and dance if you are not the one on the ladder. Enjoy the rhythms and time spent with your family.

69+1 Ways to enjoy your life during a
pandemic quarantine and to preserve your
mental health

20. Watch video segments on Instagram, WorldstarHiphop, YouTube, TicToc, Facebook, etc

Laughter is said to be a natural medicine and I've read others referring to it as God's medicine for us. To all of the people who make funny or goofy videos, thank you. For those who watch the video segments, don't take any of it seriously or personally. Just laugh your head off. You can do this and have lots of fun. Enjoy this activity alone or with others.

69+1 Ways to enjoy your life during a pandemic quarantine and to preserve your mental health

21. Pull up Youtube or an exercise app to watch and participate in some exercise

I spoke with someone recently who said, "I don't like to exercise". I thought to myself, but you have health concerns. I wasn't judging but I was thinking about how exercise helps to reduce stress, promotes a good blood pressure, done with a proper diet reduces weight, extends our lives, reduces mild depression and mild anxiety and more. Don't sleep on exercise. Get woke and get your exercise on. You can do this. For many people who never had a chance, you can do it now. There is nothing holding you back.

22. *Tell Alexa or Google home to put on your favorite dance music and go to work-dancing*

Let me be honest, I unplug my Google Home because it has responded to me to give information that I didn't ask for when it was plugged in. So, when you want to dance or hear the news instead of looking at it, plug it in and ask for what you want. "Hey Google, play Michael Jackson on YouTube." The rest is history as I go into, I know I was born to be a singer and Solid Gold dancer mode.

69+1 Ways to enjoy your life during a pandemic quarantine and to preserve your mental health

23. Teach your child, mate or parent something new

While I imagine that parents love their kids but are thoroughly frustrated to have their kids home all day during school time, as my dad used to always say, "Make the best out of a bad situation". In this situation, it's critical to create structure for your kids day or they will run a muck. So, a good balance of lessons would include technology (for learning), play, snacks, hands-on learning, and something creative. For those of you who have never wanted to be in education, just look up school schedules or for the younger kids, daycare/preschool schedules online. Though it isn't your profession, who's to say that you can't be a great one. Also, consistency is the key.

If you don't have kids, learning something new can be really cool. I remember an uncle of mine taking up the guitar in his 40's. It can be pottery, baking, letter writing, stamp collecting, drawing, sewing or whatever your heart

69+1 Ways to enjoy your life during a pandemic quarantine and to preserve your mental health

desires. If it makes you feel good, is positive and healthful for you and your family, go for it!

69+1 Ways to enjoy your life during a
pandemic quarantine and to preserve your
mental health

24. Wash, fold and put up your clothes

You could be thinking, "I do this already". Have you ever made it more interesting intentionally? Have you always shared the chore with others in the home? If not, you could do a chore lottery. Write down the chores and fold up the pieces of paper. Put them in a container and have everyone pick a chore. You can do the chore lottery each Sunday. This way everyone gets to have a different chore.

25. Reach out to people you've wronged and apologize

This might not sound like fun, but it might help with your karma and chakra. What do you think? Maybe you used to be a bully and there are some people you owe apologies to. Perhaps you played with someone's heart or mind and later on realized that you were wrong. It could be that you stole something from someone and you want to make things right. This is a good time to get your karma together. Maybe you didn't pay child support or just ghosted your child altogether. Whatever it was, clean your slate and start life anew.

69+1 Ways to enjoy your life during a pandemic quarantine and to preserve your mental health

26. *Reach out to people you haven't spoken to in a while and have a meaningful conversation*

You remember those friends you had in elementary, middle school or high school. Reach out to them. Contact them on FaceBook and get their numbers. Call a different one each day. Reminisce on the good times and talk about what you've got going on now. Let them know how much you appreciated them during that time in your life. This can be so much fun.

69+1 Ways to enjoy your life during a
pandemic quarantine and to preserve your
mental health

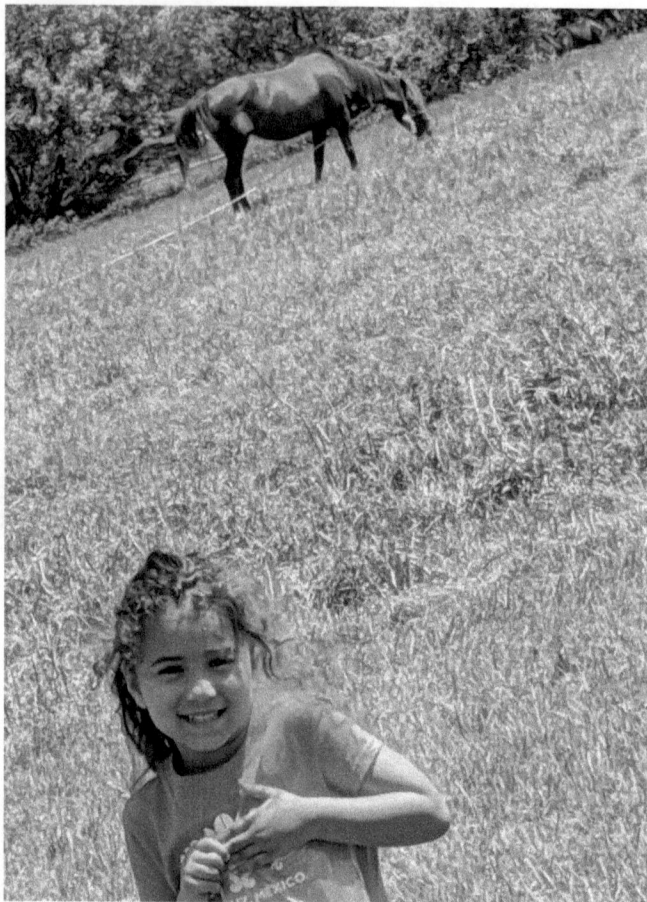

69+1 Ways to enjoy your life during a
pandemic quarantine and to preserve your
mental health

27. Start your morning with an inspirational video to set the course for the day

I'm just saying, this is the best thing since
Alexa and Google Home. Some people wake
up and start moving quickly and their entire day
is like a race. That isn't very healthy for our
minds or bodies. It's good to start the morning
in a relaxed way and that can include some
form of exercise. One of the most important
things in your day is your morning routine.
What is your morning routine composed of? Do
you listen to inspirational videos? They could
focus your mind and set your course for the
day. Try it, you'll love it. Some of the videos are
better than others, mind you, you are listening,
not necessarily watching them.

69+1 Ways to enjoy your life during a pandemic quarantine and to preserve your mental health

28. Take a nice hot bath with some epsom salt and some candles while sitting back listening to some jazz music or relaxing music of your choice

All of these put together are ultra relaxing. If you've ever had a rough day or a day where you just wanted to put all that wasn't great behind you, this is the best. I'm not sure how it feels in cool or cold water. I love warm/hot water. You can also freeze some grapes to eat while you're relaxing in the bath as well. I think that you'll enjoy this.

69+1 Ways to enjoy your life during a pandemic quarantine and to preserve your mental health

29. Create a new and meaningful way to give thanks to all of the people on the frontlines of the virus like doctors, nurses, Instacart workers, Amazon and other shipping workers, the truck drivers who deliver goods, the people working in the restaurants and at stores to make sure we can still have what we need, the people at all of the utility companies and countless others

I would say that this one needs no explanation, but then I lie. Here I was, just running my business as usual. I had been hearing about the Coronavirus on the news through various forms of media and also through clients I have in the U.K., Japan, China and other countries. So, I had just decided to switch all of my clients that I would usually see in person to online clients. Everyone was on board. Soon after, I began to get calls from others who wanted counseling but were demanding to see me in person. I had to tell these possible clients that I understood what they wanted but that wouldn't be possible. Having some inside or other

69+1 Ways to enjoy your life during a pandemic quarantine and to preserve your mental health

country-epicenter information, I had to protect myself, my family and any potential clients. None of them decided to become clients because they wanted to see me in person. As a front line person, it's important that I make solid decisions for safety. People are putting their lives on the line daily to protect us. We should be doing some positive and worthwhile things to let them know that they are appreciated. I truly appreciate Stephen Colbert and the other late night greats for working so hard to still entertain and inform us.

69+1 Ways to enjoy your life during a pandemic quarantine and to preserve your mental health

I wonder who's in charge here.

30. Take a leisurely stroll and take in nature, take pictures, pick fruit, breathe and relax

You will see some of my Google Pixel 3 photos throughout the book. They aren't professional, but I took them during some of my walks. I hope they inspire you to do the same.

69+1 Ways to enjoy your life during a pandemic quarantine and to preserve your mental health

31. Print out "All about me" worksheets offline and give them to family members. Complete them and share. I bet you learn some new things about each other.

Because of technology, we live together but are worlds apart. This type of activity can draw a family closer. If you can think of a few other activities like this, please feel free to share with me so that I can update the book. If you share it, it means to me that you're okay with freely sharing so that I can use the information to inform and help others.

You can even extend it to an "All about me video chat party".

69+1 Ways to enjoy your life during a pandemic quarantine and to preserve your mental health

32. Hold an open mic session via Zoom, Skype or other video conference platform

Enough said. Get to lyrical work- poets and rappers. Make it happen. Maybe set something up for your kids class with their teacher. That could be cool. If the kids could see each other perform or show off their projects. Love it!!

33. Start a garden with the seeds in the fruit you already have and will be eating this week

My daughter has this green thumb that I believe she got from my grandmother. I believe this because my grandmother had one. I just have a brown thumb. While I am good at growing people-let's just say plants and I are mere acquaintances that look in the opposite direction when either approaches. I've noticed that this activity has been relaxing for her just as it was for my grandmother. She was 93 when she passed in 2019, but she left the green thumbed legacy.

69+1 Ways to enjoy your life during a
pandemic quarantine and to preserve your
mental health

34. Begin a list of new positive habits to begin or habits you want to break and create plans for each then execute

In case you're stumped on this one, you can call some friends to ask about hobbies they have. If you're not interested in what they're doing, perhaps you can Google, "Fun hobbies", "Hobbies I can do for cheap" and phrases like that. You are bound to find something that interests you. If you try something that you find isn't all that it was cracked up to be, move on to the next idea.

35. Use fruits or vegetables to create diy paints

My daughter shared this idea with me. You will totally have to look this one up online. When I don't know something, I go silent… Now, dropping the mic.

69+1 Ways to enjoy your life during a
pandemic quarantine and to preserve your
mental health

69+1 Ways to enjoy your life during a pandemic quarantine and to preserve your mental health

69+1 Ways to enjoy your life during a pandemic quarantine and to preserve your mental health

36. Try the things that you think you aren't good at, prove yourself wrong

We all have self doubts sometimes. If you've ever talked yourself out of doing something that was of interest to you, you should try it. What's holding you back now? Is it something positive or fun? Try it. Ask family members to explore it with you. Try something new that isn't hurtful or harmful to you. I bet you'll have a blast.

37. Attempt to create a new joke each day to share with family and friends or watch videos of your favorite comedians and just crack up-in a good way.

Laugh from the bottom of your belly. This could also be competitive. Each person in the house or you and some friends can try to come up with the best joke daily or weekly. The person who gets the most laughs wins.

69+1 Ways to enjoy your life during a
pandemic quarantine and to preserve your
mental health

38. Think about something you could create that would help others who are on the front lines

Some people were recently making masks. What can you do? This is something huge. Other companies have repurposed themselves totally without being asked by the government to keep their employees working and to give to the people of their states and communities. Maybe this is a conversation that you can have with your friends and perhaps jointly you can do something special. This book is something special, from me to the world-during a trying time.

39. Spend time on the Freerice, Duolingo or Lumosity app

Increase your brain power. I'm sure there are others. I've personally enjoyed these. This is really something for individual growth and quiet time. Remember the saying about "Survival of the fittest", coined by Herbert Spencer. If you won't invest in you, why should others?

69+1 Ways to enjoy your life during a pandemic quarantine and to preserve your mental health

40. Begin journaling about the good, the bad and the ugly or just about your moods

For many people across the globe, journaling has been a source of reducing stress by getting certain thoughts, ideas and experiences off of one's mind. It's been said to be quite therapeutic. I'm not suggesting journaling instead of a great therapist, I'm suggesting some journaling to go along with your great therapist. Some people use a standard notebook while others buy fancy colorful, leather bound ones with a lock. It's up to you, but another way to do it is to use the speech device in Google Docs to record your journal. It has a similar benefit as saying whatever you are saying to someone. In other words, you can get your feelings off of your chest if you do it that way.

69+1 Ways to enjoy your life during a pandemic quarantine and to preserve your mental health

41. Decorate your home so that it is in feng shui

In our lives, it helps when things are decent and in order. You should have light in your home and open spaces. That is only a small part of feng shui. You should look it up or maybe even buy a book about it. It's a good book to study with friends.

69+1 Ways to enjoy your life during a pandemic quarantine and to preserve your mental health

42. Do an internal body cleanse

Since I went to Keto, all of my systems have worked impeccably. While Keto isn't for everyone, it is really a lifesaver. Keto isn't a cleanse in once sense, but for me I was able to remove foods from my diet that were causing me stomach issues that weren't really issues. It was just the everyday foods I was eating. There are many different cleanses. You can research some online. For me, I like intermittent fasting. I like to go 18 hours between meals for 3 or 4 days in a row. Talk about a well oiled machine.

43. Clean out your closet and make a pile to donate to others

This is definitely a season for giving back. Go through your closets or the space where you keep your clothes. If you haven't worn something in a year, put it in the donation bag. Drop it off to Pennywise or Salvation Army, some place that gives back to the community. Perhaps a homeless shelter or somewhere like that. Please only donate recently washed clothes without stains or tears.

44. This just in: Some YMCA's are giving free classes online

My daughter just came in and said, "Mom, the Y is giving free classes online". At this moment she is in the living room working out. That is so cool. This particular one she is watching is in Houston Texas, but I bet other Y's are getting on board too. Recommit to your goals for the new year. The Y is in it with you to win it. Spend this time refining yourself, becoming the best version of yourself! This is your time!

45. Create a list of positive affirmations to say 3 times per day to get you headed in the right direction

Sometimes we feel like we aren't meeting our goals or getting where we really want to go. One thing about that is that what we think influences every aspect of who we are. It is imperative that we replace negative thoughts with positive ones. It would be beneficial to create a list of positive affirmations (thoughts that you need to be true in your life to get where you want to go). They need to be stated positively (nothing negative in them at all). Write them down. Record them in your phone. Put them on your mirror. Say them and or listen to them at least three times per day. Purpose yourself in doing good and great things. This technique has worked for many and with your consistency, it will work for you

46. Find new ways to recycle

Since we are trying to be safe and keep others in our households safe, one of the things we can do is to find ways to recycle. This can cause us to spend less money on things when we can repurpose other items for. Spend some time online looking up ways to reuse items that would usually saturate the landfill like plastics, milk cartons and more. This can cut down on waste, the weight of the garbage that we have to throw out would decrease. This would be good for the environment and the atmosphere as a whole.

69+1 Ways to enjoy your life during a
pandemic quarantine and to preserve your
mental health

69+1 Ways to enjoy your life during a
pandemic quarantine and to preserve your
mental health

47. Plan a weekly family game/movie night or 3 depending on whose at home

Plan a weekly family game night or movie night. You can do games in the yard (bobbing for apples, hacky sack, potato sack races, soccer), board games, games using technology or other types of games. Also, a different person can choose the game or the movie for the week. No one gets to sit out. This is family time at its best. Make sure to have some chicken quesadillas, and all of the sides-sour cream, guac and more to make the night right. For those of you who like to know how things are going down, put it on a schedule or a board so everyone will know what's coming up or what's going down. Lol.

69+1 Ways to enjoy your life during a pandemic quarantine and to preserve your mental health

48. Pray to your higher power and spend some time in The Word

Many of us pray and spend that private time communing with "the powers that be". This is something that is very private and personal. Some set up an altar in their home while others pray in bed and others pray 3 times a day at specified times. Either way, get your prayer time in. With all of the things going on across the globe, this is a good time to start praying or to pray even more than usual. Read your Bible. For people who need to have it read, many computers have accessibility options that will read Bible.com aloud. You'll have to pull up the site and adjust your settings to have it read aloud.

69+1 Ways to enjoy your life during a
pandemic quarantine and to preserve your
mental health

49. Order some take out to support local businesses (or go pick it up)

Know your stores before you order. There is a
shopkeeper of the Outback which is several
miles from me. His name is Lyle. He is a very
kind gentleman. Many years ago, I was putting
on a fashion show and donating proceeds to
children in the Alief School District. Lyle was so
kind to share some incentives to support the
event. He didn't know me at all. He didn't
second guess me. In the past few weeks, I
have ordered from him 3 times. He has a big
heart and invests back into his community.
Why wouldn't I invest back into him and his
employees. I appreciate people like Lyle. He
wanted no glory, he was just being kind.

50. Make a family movie using your current technology

Each piece of technology has its own capabilities. You can write a script for one or even include friends and family who live in other places. You could collaborate on the scripts, take turns filming from different locations, another person could be responsible for the production aspect and everyone could discuss lighting and sound. This could be awesome. If it turns out good enough, perhaps you can share it on YouTube as your Pandemic Quarantine Video. Make magic with your family and friends.

69+1 Ways to enjoy your life during a
pandemic quarantine and to preserve your
mental health

51. Watch church on tv or via the internet

There is nothing like going to church in person.
I remember looking for a church with my ex
husband, D.T. We had found this church online
that seemed to fit what we were looking for.
That morning as we got prepared to go to
church, we were really happy and excited to
visit. Once we got there, we found seats and
patiently awaited what would come next. When
it was time for the sermon, the pastor was on a
screen. I was a bit dismayed. We took
showers, did hair, I put on makeup, we used
gas money and put miles on our car to watch a
pastor on a screen. "Oh No!" That wasn't the
worst. We left that church hoping to find a
church with a pastor. We pulled into another
parking lot. My husband went in to check it out.
He came running out and eagerly reported to
me about someone in the church holding a
snake in their hands at the front of the church.

So, after all of that, we just went back home to
watch Joyce Meyer online. We could have
done that in the first place. Joyce could not see
if I had on makeup or not. She wouldn't know if

69+1 Ways to enjoy your life during a pandemic quarantine and to preserve your mental health

I was eating breakfast while listening to her. And, the money I saved from not having to drive, could have been donated to the ministry. There are plenty of pastors or other ministry leaders online and on television. Remember, tithe to them like you would if you were in church. Which online church will it be for you today?

69+1 Ways to enjoy your life during a pandemic quarantine and to preserve your mental health

69+1 Ways to enjoy your life during a pandemic quarantine and to preserve your mental health

52. Have a Bible study via the the phone or internet

Many people are saddened by not being able to get out to church or be able to praise and worship in the house of the Lord. This is a grand opportunity to contact family and friends to study the Bible together online. It would be really fun if different people would lead each time. It's nice getting to hear what others think about the Bible scriptures. Though we all read the same words, we can interpret it differently. Please, be kind during this process.
Sometimes we can feel like we know more. That doesn't mean to force your perspectives down the throats of others. Let this be a time of joy and unification. Let this be a time to learn more about God and each other. Study in love.

69+1 Ways to enjoy your life during a
pandemic quarantine and to preserve your
mental health

53. Have a family reunion via the internet with the all the fixings and music

My grandmother, Leola B. Hughes and my grandfather, Fred Hughes used to take me all over the country for family reunions. My father, Johnny "B. Good" Augillard would take me to our family reunions as well. The best things about them were the people and the food. There were many fun activities like bounce houses, ring toss, talent shows, museums visits, churches and more. We enjoyed crawfish boils, wonderful barbeque and so much more. We made memories. I challenge you to set up a family reunion online with your family and send pictures or video with the hashtag #FamilyReunion@TheTrahanTherapyCenter on instagram. This is a huge opportunity to get some of your normalcy back. Each family can prepare good food, play Maze or some other dynamic music, prepare for games online and in person with the people they live with. I'll be looking for your #'s.

69+1 Ways to enjoy your life during a pandemic quarantine and to preserve your mental health

54. Write a family history to put together to share with the family and family yet to be born

54 and 55 can go hand in hand. For those who like to organize pictures and the like, they can work on number 55. For people who like to do research and organize family information by dates, last names, marriages, look at wellness and illness factors, where they were born and when they died, this will be another collaborative activity. You can start with what you do know and then reach out to other family members who are willing to do a FaceTime call to work on the project together. When you have gotten as far as you can go on your own, you might consider Ancestry or a company like that to be able to dig deeper to be able to create a more in depth project.

69+1 Ways to enjoy your life during a pandemic quarantine and to preserve your mental health

55. Create a collage of family pics, places you want to go or things you'd like to achieve

Some people live in families where they never get to meet grandparents and great grandparents. With extra time on your hands, now is a good time to put together a paper/electronic scrapbook. You can make a cover. You can send it to family members. Family members in different states can collaborate and send or add additional photos. You can also add stickers and emojis and add people names, where they were born and possibly even family trees. This would be an awesome family activity.

69+1 Ways to enjoy your life during a pandemic quarantine and to preserve your mental health

56. Play video games online

I should really allow my son or others to speak about this. In the past I've had students who've raved about this. This is something millions of people across the globe enjoy. If you do, enjoy this along with many other fun things on this list. Connect with friends and compete. Maybe each person can take a turn choosing to give a prize like a gift card, a baseball hat or something like that. It's not about gambling, it's about people competing and getting something out of their winning. Don't offer more than something valued at more than $10 bucks. It's all in fun. Make it a great time.

69+1 Ways to enjoy your life during a
pandemic quarantine and to preserve your
mental health

57. If you're on payroll, even your own-do a little work

Working from home can prove to be tough because now all you need to go out for is nothing. You can order groceries online and everything else. So, many of us have a mate, kids or grandkids or a roommate which means a cooperative situation. You might have to establish boundaries such as quiet time or when you absolutely can't be bothered. Do your best to ensure that your work space has a lot of light (unless you're a photographer), perhaps a plant and some music in the background that can add to your productivity. You know how you work best, just prepare for success. If you were in the midst of starting your own business prior to this calamity, put your head down and forge ahead. Or maybe you were working on some business plans for the future. Continue your research. You can do this!

69+1 Ways to enjoy your life during a pandemic quarantine and to preserve your mental health

69+1 Ways to enjoy your life during a pandemic quarantine and to preserve your mental health

58. Sit on the sofa with a throw, a glass of wine (18+) and popcorn while enjoying a good movie

Is anything more relaxing? Do you have a comfy couch with big squishy pillows? If not, add some pillows from your bed to it. Make popcorn for yourself or the gang with some Honest Kids or Capri Sun juices for the kids. If you want to do it up a little more, perhaps the kids like TGIF potato boats or some wings with ranch. The main thing is to get to the couch and enjoy a lovely movie, alone or with family-laugh together, cry together. Just appreciate every breath, every moment. Don't forget to put your smart tv on surround sound like you're at the theater. Happy couching.

69+1 Ways to enjoy your life during a
pandemic quarantine and to preserve your
mental health

59. Clip your ends or cut your hair since the salon is closed, tighten up the weave

Just because the salon is closed, we don't have to look like little monsters running all over the place. Please wash and condition your hair and clip your ends. Also, don't wear the weave past the wearable state. If you don't have more weave, please just take it out and wash the beautiful locks that grew from your scalp and style them beautifully. Guys, if you don't know what to do, look online and do your best. If all else fails, just cut it very low.

69+1 Ways to enjoy your life during a pandemic quarantine and to preserve your mental health

60. Paint that room that's been needing a new coat

You can clean the walls, paint the walls or other honey do's around the house. It's the place where you live and perhaps it could use some touch-ups. By the way, most hardware stores sell touch-up paint. Did I not put, clean your ceiling fans on the list? Lol. Now you have it. Please clean your ceiling fans. This is good for general hygiene and for anyone with upper respiratory/asthma issues.

69+1 Ways to enjoy your life during a pandemic quarantine and to preserve your mental health

61. Ride your bicycle, your Peloton or jump onto the treadmill, hit those squats

Yes, exercise again. Each person enjoys a different type of exercise. It doesn't matter which you prefer but as our former First Lady, Michelle Obama said, "Let's move!" She's such a tough act to follow, but I digress. Choose a time of day that is good for you, ride with family or alone. Maintain your social distance. Just have fun. Of course you can compete with the Peloton or the treadmill. You can compete to see who burns the most calories in a certain period of time. Enjoy it. Make it fun.

69+1 Ways to enjoy your life during a
pandemic quarantine and to preserve your
mental health

62. *Love and make love to your mate but also, give them some space to promote peace*

Make peace, not war. Love your mate. Treat them with kindness and respect. Be patient with your mate and don't take advantage of your mate's patience. "We were so happy when we both went to work, but now one of us is laid off and the other is working from home." This script is playing out across the globe. Don't become a pandemic divorce statistic. Take your space and give your partner or other family members space. If this means going to your room, hanging out in the garage, the backyard on the patio or the porch, take some space from others and give them some space. That is the whole purpose in this book. Find ways to be entertained independently or with others.

69+1 Ways to enjoy your life during a
pandemic quarantine and to preserve your
mental health

69+1 Ways to enjoy your life during a pandemic quarantine and to preserve your mental health

63. Draw or paint a beautiful picture, sculpt a beautiful piece

Beauty is in the eye of the beholder. That's what I learned while growing up. Online and in bookstores you can find books that teach you how to draw one line at a time. If you're an artist already, you won't need that. Perhaps a canvas, brushes, paint, pencils and the proper erasers might be a good start. For the novices, it isn't about a perfect picture, it's more about making something that you perceive as beautiful. You can do this. If the kids are doing it too, establish a space for them, cover the floor and don't give them anything to manage on their own (under age 7) that could spill.

64. Sit in your office or near a window to watch the birds, squirrels and nature

Your terrain may be different, but from many windows you will see such a variety of things. Maybe you will see a bear or an aardvark. It might be big cars or little cars and one car cutting off another. Maybe you'll notice the sway of the trees as the wind blows the long and curvy branches. Whatever it is in nature, relax, be mindful and enjoy the moments.

69+1 Ways to enjoy your life during a pandemic quarantine and to preserve your mental health

65. Create a music playlist from every genre you enjoy

You know what this is about. Perhaps one for jazz, one for the 80's and 90's another one for classical, one for hip hop, country, rock and roll and rhythm and blues. I know those aren't the only playlists you could make, but these would be some cool listens.

69+1 Ways to enjoy your life during a pandemic quarantine and to preserve your mental health

66. Learn to cook without power on a cast iron pan with rocks and wood

Cousin Mary shared this one. Yes, it's good to have skills in the event something happens and the power we all rely upon isn't working. What would you do today if your electricity went out? How would you cook? How would you survive?

69+1 Ways to enjoy your life during a pandemic quarantine and to preserve your mental health

67. Take a nap

So, my cousin Lee gave me this one. He said that his grandmother, Elmer Lois always told him about the importance of a nap when he was growing up. Once we grow up, we are told that kids take naps, not grown ups. It's hard for me to take one, but even a 15-20 minute power nap can do you a world of good.

69+1 Ways to enjoy your life during a pandemic quarantine and to preserve your mental health

68. Put together a puzzle

My grandfather, Fred Hughes used to love putting together puzzles and for him it was quite relaxing. While he enjoyed putting puzzles together, my mother enjoyed word searches. Of course, if you live in the U.S., you might have heard of some of the famous puzzles in the New York Times. The idea is to find the type of puzzle you like and enjoy it alone or with family. Don't be puzzled, be the puzzler.

69+1 Ways to enjoy your life during a pandemic quarantine and to preserve your mental health

69. Listen to a book or podcast

When I was in school , everything was in a book. We read so many books. We had that standard set of encyclopedias and an old Webster's dictionary. I am not old enough to have experienced the stories they used to tell on the radio. Nowadays we can listen to books online and listen to interesting interviews and individual takes on different topics via a podcast. You can learn a variety of information via audiobooks and podcasts.

69+1 Ways to enjoy your life during a
pandemic quarantine and to preserve your
mental health

70. Crochet or similar yarn work

I don't know how this almost slipped from my mind. My grandmother would spend endless hours crocheting or knitting. She made my Godchild's christening gown and cap. It was so beautiful. The yarn was white, had a sheen to it and you would have sworn that it was a $400 outfit. People make various types of clothing for the home and their families and even for the homeless through crocheting and knitting. If you don't know how, there are many books on Amazon and in Barnes & Nobles about how to do it and certainly there are many videos on YouTube and other sites. This can be quite relaxing and you can even make money from your output. Could this be for you?

69+1 Ways to enjoy your life during a pandemic quarantine and to preserve your mental health

71. *Create an app that can be meaningful during times like these or just to help solve a global problem.*

We have so many apps and it's often a challenge deciding which to choose to download. Just because there are a lot doesn't mean that there isn't room for some more meaningful apps that can solve problems and help society as a whole. You might have a great idea that should be shared via the app medium. There are free platforms on which to build an app. Try it today.

72. Build a fort
73. Take a boat ride using social distancing
74. Jump on your trampoline
75. Make soap or bath bombs from scratch
76. Dye your hair
77. Encourage others
78. Give like you want others to give to you
79. Cry if you need to
80. Just breathe through it

69+1 Ways to enjoy your life during a
pandemic quarantine and to preserve your
mental health

69+1 Ways to enjoy your life during a pandemic quarantine and to preserve your mental health

Children's Trauma

While children don't know the language of trauma, changing their routines without warning can cause them to feel unsafe. Routines and consistency allow children to feel secure. Children across the globe don't fully understand what's going on in the world right now. They miss their friends and even the teachers they weren't fond of.

Having parents in the household who are helping them to cope is beneficial. Having family activities that use energy is important to reduce the anxiety of everyone in the home. Turning off the news and turning on music is better.

Show your children love, care, concern and compassion at this time. Though many things aren't our usual right now, try to create a solid routine to reinstill that need for security into the children.

If they cry more easily, become frustrated more easily or begin to demonstrate any signs like

69+1 Ways to enjoy your life during a pandemic quarantine and to preserve your mental health

those that aren't consistent with who they were prior to the coronavirus 19, please give them support, space and time. Most of all, don't scream and holler at them. With the reinstatement of safety, they will self-regulate more.

Once life returns to what's considered within the scope of normal, if your child fails to adjust you might want to seek out play therapy, music therapy or just psychotherapy to help them to process all that has happened and their feelings.

69+1 Ways to enjoy your life during a pandemic quarantine and to preserve your mental health

Other tips

<u>Protocols to put in place if you are still having to leave home to work with others:</u>
- Wash your hands at every opportunity
- Keep your safe distance (6 feet) away from others
- Keep your own personal sanitizer to use
- Use gloves when touching others or things others have touched
- Use gloves when getting into your car and discard them after you have disrobed at home
- When you get home, if you have a garage: disrobe down to your underwear in the garage then head straight into the shower.
- If you don't have a garage, have a space in your home, right next to the door to disrobe and put your clothes in a bag to dump them into a washer then jump into the shower
- When done go back to clean light switches, door handles, washing machine buttons or knobs

69+1 Ways to enjoy your life during a
pandemic quarantine and to preserve your
mental health

- When you are about to enter your car
  again, clean the door handle, the
  steering wheel and other buttons that
  you might have touched the day before
- If you believe that you have experienced
  some of these symptoms but are now
  over it, it might be a good idea to take
  an antibody test

69+1 Ways to enjoy your life during a pandemic quarantine and to preserve your mental health

In closing, I hope that this book has stimulated your mind and has caused you to maybe pick up an old instrument, to take some beautiful pictures or has even inspired you to get to know your family again. In this age of technology, we have really gotten away from knowing and really loving each other. We are more distant now than 30 years ago. This book is about you keeping things together, staying sane, getting to know yourself better. Love, learn, live and enjoy your life one day at a time. Enjoy and appreciate the little things. And, it's funny, I saw that a few companies have put together this virtual dating online. I'm wondering if we shouldn't have been there already.

69+1 Ways to enjoy your life during a pandemic quarantine and to preserve your mental health

Special thanks go to: My daughter who shared several ideas about how to enjoy life. My cousins Mary Ellen and Lee W. for sharing specific ideas of what's important to them. My granddaughter for her natural poses. To my son who gave me guidance on the cover design. Thanks to all of the professional photographers for not judging my novice photographs.

www.ingramcontent.com/pod-product-compliance
Lightning Source LLC
Chambersburg PA
CBHW070640030426
42337CB00020B/4103